I0148547

Conde Benoist Pallen

New Rubaiyat

Conde Benoist Pallen

New Rubaiyat

ISBN/EAN: 9783742801234

Manufactured in Europe, USA, Canada, Australia, Japa

Cover: Foto ©Andreas Hilbeck / pixelio.de

Manufactured and distributed by brebook publishing software
(www.brebook.com)

Conde Benoist Pallen

New Rubaiyat

NEW RUBÁIYÁT

BY

CONDÉ BENOIST PALLEN.

Faith and unfaith can ne'er be equal powers:
Unfaith in aught is want of faith in all.

Tennyson.

Printed for B. Herder
Publisher, 17 South
Broadway, St. Louis,
Missouri. MDCCCXCVIII.

Preface. ✣✣✣✣✣

Edoward Fitzgerald's translation of the Rubáiyát of Omar Khayyám, introduced the modern world to the scepticism of the Poet-Astronomer of Persia and placed his quatrains amongst the classics of English verse. The thoroughly sceptical temper of the Rubáiyát with its epicurean reflex so aptly chimes with the unfaith of the present century, that in Fitzgerald's admirable rendition it would seem to be the very voice of modern doubt itself, instead of the mediæval utterance of a poet who sang and died a century before Dante. The unfaith of to-day boasts itself peculiar and sole; Omar Khayyám's scepticism cancels the modern presumption, and we see in his Rubáiyát the same garment about the shoulders of a mediæval doubter in the Orient as hides the nakedness of the modern unbeliever in the Occident.

The quatrains which I here presume to publish are written in a spirit quite different from Omar's scepticism. Their burden is Faith, and their purpose to show that not only is unfaith a false and hopeless screed, but that the reason and soul of man find their interior and exterior harmony only when attuned to the key-note of Faith. As the new quatrains constantly keep Omar's Rubáiyát* in view, I have appended Fitzgerald's translation (first edition) to assist the reader's understanding.

*Verses or Stanzas.

NEW RUBÁIYÁT.

Old Omar, subtle weaver of the skein
Of doubt entangled in thy perplexed brain,
    In that far East which saw thine ancient day,
This later hour awakes thy voice again,

And in a newer tongue recasts the phrase
That doubled glibly in thine olden ways,
    On life and death and those dark questionings,
Which doubt may answer not, though doubt may
        raise.

This newer vase that holds thine ancient wine,
Is rich with lines as gracious as were thine,
    As delicately graved, as feetly traced
With clinging tendril of the worshiped vine.

Nor deem I that the pouring of thy song
From old to newer vessel does thee wrong,
    For bold the hand that fashioned the new clay,
A master's hand, and as a master's, strong.

Nor strange that he should seek thine unfaith out,
Who felt a fellow sympathy in doubt,
  In this his day when creeds have crumbled down,
Blown like the dust of simoons round about.

For that old plaint which sickened thy soft soul,
And to thy lips held up the poisoned bowl
  Made luscious with the nectars of the sense,
Still sings your song and echoes all its dole.

And though his noisy doubt the newer man
Boast as fresh light upon the marching van
   Of progress to the piping fife of change—
Your doubt was ancient ere his doubt began.

For you, as he, sing faith and unfaith's strife,
And he, as you, chants death the bourn of life;
   He now, and you a thousand years ago,
Into the heart of faith drives deep the knife.

Thy dubious hand upon the shifting scale
Touched every trembling note, drew every wail,
   Sounded each plaint and struck each quivering
      chord;
He now and you of old—to what avail?

As dark a riddle is that silent fate
To the blind sceptic of this newer date,
   As ever answered not to thy light word,
Who asked in dalliance at the outer gate.

For truth speaks only at the inner shrine,
Not in the tavern where they spill the wine,
  Pours only through the cleansed and chastened
      sense
The cryptic sweetness of the living vine.

To list thy lilting numbers' softened strain,
And hear it chiming with the rhythmed pain
  Thy later brothers plaint on modern lutes,
Wakes smiling comment on their little gain.

Alas, that you in mediæval years
Sang all their doubts, shed all their hopeless tears,
   Their creedless creed in all its changes rang,
And coined their wisdom in your ancient fears.

Science but now, they cry with echoing bruit,
Has plucked the higher wisdom's ripened fruit,
   Achieved the summit of a nobler view,
And struck in wider knowledge deeper root.

Yet all the garnered learning of the age
Has added not a tittle to your page;
    Of that first truth and last the soul desires
Your word as wise as theirs, your wit as sage.

Your wit and theirs both dark as starless night,
Searching the universe with candle light,
    Agrope within the same abyss of dread
Where depth grows black with depth and height
        with height.

In vain you sought, as vain they seek, the clue
Where doubt makes mocking shadows of the true,
   Dissolves the answer in the question's breath,
The doubt that asks from doubt that never knew.

An echo questioned back the mockery flings,
And doubt that asks of doubt with unfaith rings;
   Responsive to the fingers wail the strings,
And as you key the trembling chord, it sings.

You drew the music of your plaintive strain
From the sore grief of Philomel's sad pain,
   But dashed the sweetness of her chastened song
With doubt, and poisoned all its balm with bane.

You sang, and sadly sweet your ancient rhyme,
The fleeting footsteps of the phantom time,
   The dying sweetness of the hastening rose,
Life's transient blush undone by death's swift crime.

Yea, vanity in him, who lays up store
Of hope to reap his harvest on time's shore,
   And sewing all the fields that lie around,
Prepares the granary and the threshing floor.

Ah, swift the courses of the rushing sun,
And changeful are the glittering hours that run
   'Twixt hope's first blossom and the blown flower,
For evening sees not what the morn begun.

Yea, like a traveller from his tent he goes,
Who waits the harvest even to the close,
   For long and short within the sum of time
Are cancelled equal to the star and rose.

And Sultan Mahmud in his pomp and pride,
Though thrice three decades with his power abide,
   At last commingles with the dust of him,
Who only gasped his little life and died.

The past bears crowded witness to this truth,
That soon or late death reaps his solemn ruth
   In all mortality, and in the end
Ashes to ashes, be it age or youth.

Where Jamshyd drank, death slakes his thirsty
      throat,
Where Jamshyd gloried, slinks the creeping stoat,
   And echoing to his long-past wassail song,
The lengthening silence winds its deepening note.

And Cæsar's dust beneath a peasant's feet,
For wisdom's eloquence were theme replete,
   How leveled by the sweeping scythe of time,
Fame and unfame in one oblivion meet.

So has the ages' wisdom ever sung,
And from earth's hollow glories wailing wrung
   The tribute of its dole: not new your song
Nor new the lesson of your mellow tongue.

Though Jamshyd long has quaffed the last black
        draught,
And Cæsar, smitten by the bitter shaft
    That pricked his glory's bubble, heedless sleeps;
Their dust but shallow soil for wisdom's graft.

The rose you sing from Cæsar's clay that blows
Like Cæsar's glory for an instant shows
    And crumbles back to that from whence it bloomed;
From dust it came and unto dust it goes.

Mortal to mortal is the ancient law,
Earth back to earth again the whole world's saw:
  Mortality is written broad and deep,
And fools that run the easy lesson draw.

Yes, easy is the folly that seems wise
And cloaks short knowledge in a long disguise;
  Easy the truth that time is swift of flight,
The flower that blooms to-day, to-morrow dies.

Easy to drown, the heedless cup within,
The gruesome memory of the death and sin
   That racked the soul with their black questionings,
And as unbidden guests of old stalked in.

Nor you the first, nor last, to thrust them out
And welcome in their place a reeling rout
   Who drink and question not, but steep in floods
Of mellow vintage all the ghosts of doubt.

Brief wisdom and short triumph your poor plot
To cheat the destiny the years allot
  By drowning memory In a shallow cup;—
Though now forgetting, you are not forgot.

And while you wander in a vinous mist
Through roseate ways as your soft pleasures list,
  The spinner Time still plies his tireless loom,
And death and you are drawing to the tryst.

What answer then in that appointed place,
When he breathes cold upon your yellowing face,
    What answer echoing from the empty cup?
Regret within the lees, think you, or grace?

TO-DAY the chosen mistress of your lot
To-morrow baned and YESTERDAY forgot:—
    Lo, YESTERDAY accuses from the dead,
TO-MORROW beckons, for TO-DAY is not.

Fast running out the limit of your thread,
TO-DAY and YESTERDAY forever sped;
 The whirling loom roars distantly and faint,
And all your years are ashes with the dead.

So careful of the present and its joys
Hoarding as children all the broken toys;
 The little wrecks now strew the dusty floor,
And you forgotten with your childish noise.

So careful now within your eager hands
That not a grain shall waste of time's swift sands—
   The very grain you clench has trickled through ;
TO-DAY holds not what YESTERDAY demands.

TO-DAY but borrows what TO-MORROW lends,
And pays to YESTERDAY what now it spends,
   And debtor still with nothing of its own
A bankrupt in the hands of Death it ends.

Why stake on nothingness the all you own,
And cast life's ashes to the whirlwind blown?
   He loses time who builds on time alone,
And nothing shall be reaped from nothing sown.

What boot the pleasures of a century's run,
If all their sweets but end where they begun,
   In that swift nothing of an instant's flight,
A prize that's lost before the prize is won.

The years gone down into the gaping tomb
Of Yesterday are dream wastes in the gloom,
  Dim wraiths of time embraced but never held,
Visions that stare from out an ancient room.

Sum up their all and hoard your empty gain ;
Hope crushed by fear, joy strangled in the pain,
  Life touched by death at every baffled turn,
Dying to live and then to die again.

And when upon the darkened verge you stand
Where life's faint stream is lost in death's quick sand,
    What garnered treasure do the senses hold?
An eyeless skull within a nerveless hand.

Who turns all things to uses of the sense
Shall glean in sense his only recompense,
    And time abused shall be by time avenged;
Life sewn in death shall reap in impotence.

*   *   *   *   *   *   *   *

You tell us that you turned from Wisdom's door,
Sifting the heaped-up rubbish on the floor
    Of learning's vestibule, but found no key:—
And was the portal locked—are you so sure?

Think you that thus the road to Wisdom lies,
And on the rungs of knowledge men may rise
    To that pure empyrean, as small boys.
Plant little ladders to essay the skies?

Not all the gleaning of the laboring West,
Nor all the knowledge of the Orient's quest
  May scale a single inch of that far height:
Who seeketh not is he who seeketh best.

Knowledge may reach from shining star to star,
Enthroned on seven-ringed Saturn sit afar,
  And still as distant be from Wisdom's house
As when it beat against this lower bar.

The door to which in vain *your* key you plied,
The door you found so tightly sealed, stands wide
  To him who bends in leal humility:
He enters not who walks erect in pride.

You thought to compass with your little span
The wide abysses of creation's plan,
  And finite measure infinite design ;
You—you would be God, who are but man.

Believe th' Omniscient, who ordained the law,
The end as well as the beginning saw;
   Trust thou th' Omnipotent, who made the whole,
O'errules it all: not His but yours the flaw.

Heaven but countersigns your own decree,
And as you sew your years so shall they be:
   This much of fate is true, that as you plant,
So shall you pluck the fruitage of the tree.

The daring mind that seeks to wholly sift
The heart of mystery, may never lift
   The veil that hides her face from prying eyes:
From Wisdom's hand you cannot wrest her gift.

Who would unchastely pierce her secret pale
Shall find her panoplied in hardest mail;
   Who seeks to violate her fane shall meet
The entrance barred and closely drawn the veil.

The gathered lightnings shall about him play,
And thunderous wrath shall fill his fearful way,
  Whose lustful eye would take her face unveiled :
The sacrilege with blindness shall he pay.

The question put, the answer comes in kind :
Who asks in simple faith in faith shall find
  The answer ; but pride re-echoes pride,
And blind the understanding of the blind. ·

Who asks of Earth, shall hear of Earth reply:
Earth born of earth in earth again shall die;
    A fugitive your little course you run,
And there return, and there forever lie.

Who asks of Heaven an unseen voice shall hear
Singing like chimings of the crystal sphere
    Of interstellar spaces ringing clear:
There a little while, forever here;

A little while to school th' impatient soul,
To read by faith the riddle of the scroll
   That Wisdom writes in hieroglyphs of time;
There the lesser part, but here the whole.

For Love gazed on the Beauty of the Face
Of His Beloved and upward welled in grace,
   As everlasting fountains pouring forth
Abundant floods make bloom a desert place.

Love in creation's wondrous mirror sought
To multiply the image of His Thought,
   And pouring forth his Power upon the void,
In Love the likeness of His Love He wrought.

And back again as surging flames aspire,
Creation lifts to Love's eternal fire ;
   Time but the rushing of her eager flight
Upon the outstretched pinions of desire;

Death, the instant of the journey done,
When all the courses of the way are run,
   The door through which departs the passing guest,
Who goes upon the rising of the sun.

For Love devised the plan and Love makes test
Of faith to that far end that Love knows best;
   And this the message Love by Wisdom sends:
In Faith abide, and leave to Love the rest.

Divorce not Reason from thy failing house
To make with concubines a vain carouse;
   But take her, prudent partner of thy years,
To cherish chastely as a faithful spouse.

She, too, is of celestial origin,
And knows how close to Faith she is akin,
   Faith, her elder sister, in whose eyes
Dissolves the secret death, the riddle, sin.

For Reason, modest in her household lore,
Seeks not beyond the threshold of her door;
   Diviner truths in Wisdom's utterance given,
Takes from the lips of Faith, and asks no more.

By Faith and Faith alone in panic rout
The misbelieving horde is driven out,
   Fate's nameless terror lifted from the soul,
Fate the echo of the voice of doubt.

Forgetfulness in sense a sorry scheme
To cheat the conscience and make seem
   The "IS" and "IS-NOT" all a phantom show,
And time the fading shadow of a dream.

For Reason drugged a thousand times and more,
A ravaged captive on the tavern floor,
   Awakes again, loathing her fallen state,
And clamors for her freedom at the door.

Though shamed and flouted victim of thy rape,
She does not die ; and you may not escape
   Her importuning voice, nor think to end
The issue in the lethe of the grape.

   *   *   *   *   *   *   *   *

Come from the stifling tavern's baleful glare
Into the sunshine and the outer air,
   With gladdened nature greeting everywhere,
And looking up to Heaven, see, how fair !

How pure the wide savannah's vaulted sweep,
One sapphire flame from glowing deep to deep;
  This crystal cup hold to thy crackled lip,
And drinking feel the freshened pulses leap.

Drink, and clear the phantoms from the brain,
Cleanse from the sluggish blood the treacherous bane
  That poisoned all the wells of life and truth ;
Drink ! Look up ! and once again be sane.

With chastened sense and in the firmer mind
Look in pure nature's eyes, and you shall find
   A secret half spelled out and half divined:
Within the emblem truth is not confined.

Her secret word a faint prefiguring;
She speaks in shadow of the higher thing,
   Like pale penumbra of the light unseen,
The sun's veiled glory from an outer ring.

Within the deepened shadow's darkened plot,
You sought the source of light and found it not;
  Your eyes grew dim with searching in the dark,
And blindness out of darkness was begot.

The shadow is but shade of hidden light;
It is the sun by earth eclipsed makes night:
  Heaven is gracious to our little power
And her far secret tempers to our sight.

The need of Faith from nature's secret learn ;
Reason from Faith and Faith from Love in turn
   Draws light and life: in One see all else rest,
And in things seen the things unseen discern.

And though thy years are drawing to their close,
And youth and spring have faded with the rose,
   Faith plucks the thorn of thy regret, and lo !
Upon the naked stem Hope's floweret blows,

And all the garden blossoms, and the Vine
Into Love's chalice pours diviner Wine:
　　Faith holds the secret of the sacred sign;
Her eyes search deep and long, and make it thine.

RUBÁIYÁT

OF

OMAR KHAYYÁM OF NÁISHÁPUR.

Translated by EDWARD FITZGERALD.

[FIRST EDITION.]

AWAKE! for Morning in the Bowl of Night
Has flung the Stone that puts the Stars to Flight:
    And Lo! the Hunter of the East has caught
The Sultan's Turret in a Noose of Light.

Dreaming, when Dawn's Left Hand was in the Sky,
I heard a Voice within the Tavern cry,
    "Awake, my Little ones, and fill the Cup
"Before Life's Liquor in its Cup be dry."

49

And, as the Cock crew, those who stood before
The Tavern shouted—"Open then the Door!
"You know how little while we have to stay,
"And, once departed, may return no more."

Now, the New Year reviving old Desires,
The thoughtful Soul to Solitude retires,
    Where the WHITE HAND OF MOSES on the Bough
Puts out, and Jesus from the Ground suspires.

Iram indeed is gone with all its Rose,
And Jamshyd's Sev'n-ring'd Cup where no one knows;
    But still the Vine her ancient Ruby yields,
And still a Garden by the Water blows.

And David's lips are lock't; but in divine
High piping Pehlevi, with "Wine! Wine! Wine!
    "*Red* Wine!"—the Nightingale cries to the Rose
That yellow Cheek of her's to 'incarnadine.

Come, fill the Cup, and in the Fire of Spring
The Winter Garment of Repentance fling:
    The Bird of Time has but a little way
To fly—and Lo! the Bird is on the Wing.

And look—a thousand Blossoms with the Day
Woke—and a thousand scatter'd into Clay:
    And this first Summer Month that brings the Rose
Shall take Jamshyd and Kaikobad away.

But come with old Khayyam, and leave the Lot
Of Kaikobad and Kaikhosru forgot:
    Let Rustum lay about him as he will,
Or Hatim Tai cry Supper—heed them not.

With me along some Strip of Herbage strown
That just divides the desert from the sown,
    Where name of Slave and Sultan scarce is known,
And pity Sultan Mahmud on his Throne.

Here with a Loaf of Bread beneath the Bough
A Flask of Wine, a Book of Verse—and Thou
    Beside me singing in the Wilderness—
And Wilderness is Paradise enow.

"How sweet is mortal Sovranty !"—think some:
Others—"How blest the Paradise to come !"
    Ah, take the Cash in hand and waive the Rest;
Oh, the brave Music of a *distant* Drum!

Look to the Rose that blows about us—"Lo,
"Laughing," she says, "into the World I blow:
    "At once the silken Tassel of my Purse
"Tear, and its Treasure on the Garden throw."

The Worldly Hope men set their Hearts upon
Turns Ashes—or it prospers; and anon,
    Like Snow upon the Desert's dusty Face
Lighting a little Hour or two—is gone.

And those who husbanded the Golden Grain,
And those who flung it to the Winds like Rain,
　　Alike to no such aureate Earth are turn'd
As, buried once, Men want dug up again.

Think, in this batter'd Caravanserai
Whose Doorways are alternate Night and Day,
　　How Sultan after Sultan with his Pomp
Abode his Hour or two, and went his way.

They say the Lion and the Lizard keep
The Courts where Jamshyd gloried and drank deep:
　　And Bahram, that great Hunter—the Wild Ass
Stamps o'er his Head, and he lies fast asleep.

I sometimes think that never blows so red
The Rose as where some buried Cæsar bled;
　　That every Hyacinth the Garden wears
Dropt in its Lap from some once lovely Head.

And this delightful Herb whose tender Green
Fledges the River's Lip on which we lean,
　　Ah, lean upon it lightly! for who knows
From what once lovely Lip it springs unseen!

Ah, my Beloved, fill the Cup that clears
TO-DAY of past Regrets and future Fears—
　　To-morrow?—Why, To-morrow I may be
Myself with Yesterday's Sev'n Thousand Years.

Lo! some we loved, the loveliest and best
That Time and Fate of all their Vintage prest,
   Have drunk their Cup a Round or two before,
And one by one crept silently to Rest.

And we, that now make merry in the Room
They left, and Summer dresses in new Bloom,
   Ourselves must we beneath the Couch of Earth
Descend, ourselves to make a Couch—for whom?

Ah, make the most of what we yet may spend,
Before we too in the Dust descend;
   Dust into Dust, and under Dust, to lie,
Sans Wine, sans Song, sans Singer, and—sans End!

Alike for those who for TO-DAY prepare,
And those that after a TO-MORROW stare,
   A Muezzin from the Tower of Darkness cries
"Fools! your Reward is neither Here nor There!"

Why, all the Saints and Sages who discuss'd
Of the Two Worlds so learnedly, are thrust
   Like foolish Prophets forth; their Words to Scorn
Are scatter'd, and their Mouths are stopt with Dust.

Oh, come with old Khayyam, and leave the Wise
To talk; one thing is certain, that Life flies;
   One thing is certain, and the Rest is lies;
The Flower that once has blown for ever dies.

Myself when young did eagerly frequent
Doctor and Saint, and heard great Argument
    About it and about: but evermore
Came out by the same Door as in I went.

With them the Seed of Wisdom did I sow,
And with my own hand labor'd it to grow:
    And this was all the Harvest that I reap'd—
"I came like Water, and like Wind I go."

Into this Universe, and *why* not knowing,
Nor *whence*, like Water willy-nilly flowing:
    And out of it, as Wind along the Waste,
I know not *whither*, willy-nilly blowing.

What, without asking, hither hurried *whence?*
And, without asking, *whither* hurried hence!
    Another and another Cup to drown
The Memory of this Impertinence!

Up from Earth's Centre through the Seventh Gate
I rose and on the Throne of Saturn sate,
    And many Knots unravel'd by the Road;
But not the Knot of Human Death and Fate.

There was a Door to which I found no Key:
There was a Veil past which I could not see:
    Some little Talk awhile of *Me* and *Thee*
There seemed—and then no more of *Thee* and *Me*.

Then to the rolling Heav'n itself I cried,
Asking, "What Lamp had Destiny to guide
    "Her little Children stumbling in the Dark?"
And—"A blind Understanding!" Heav'n replied.

Then to this earthen Bowl did I adjourn
My Lip the secret Well of Life to learn:
    And Lip to Lip it murmur'd—"While you live
"Drink!—for once dead you never shall return."

I think the Vessel, that with fugitive
Articulation answer'd, once did live.
    And merry-make; and the cold Lip I kiss'd
How many Kisses might it take—and give!

For in the Market-place, one Dusk of Day,
I watch'd the Potter thumping his wet Clay:
    And with its all obliterated Tongue   ·
It murmur'd—"Gently, Brother, gently, pray!"

Ah, fill the Cup:—what boots it to repeat
How Time is slipping underneath our Feet:
    Unborn TO-MORROW, and dead YESTERDAY,
Why fret about them if TO-DAY be sweet?

Oh, if my Soul can fling his Dust aside,
And naked on the Air of Heaven ride,
    Is't not a Shame, is't not a Shame for Him
So long in this Clay Suburb to abide?

Or is *that* but a Tent, where rests anon
A Sultan to his Kingdom passing on,
　　And which the swarthy Chamberlain shall strike
Then when the Sultan rises to be gone?

One Moment in Annihilation's Waste,
One Moment, of the Well of Life to taste—
　　The Stars are setting and the Caravan
Starts for the Dawn of Nothing—Oh, make haste!

How long, how long, in infinite Pursuit
Of This and That endeavour and dispute?
　　Better be merry with the fruitful Grape,
Than sadden after none, or bitter, Fruit.

You know, my Friends, how long since in my House
For a new Marriage I did make Carouse:
　　Divorced old barren Reason from my Bed,
And took the Daughter of the Vine to Spouse.

For "IS" and "IS NOT" though with Rule and Line,
And "UP-AND-DOWN" *without*, I could define,
　　I yet in all I only cared to know;
Was never deep in anything but—Wine.

And lately, by the Tavern Door agape,
Came stealing through the Dusk an Angel Shape
　　Bearing a Vessel on his Shoulder; and
He bid me taste of it; and 't was—the Grape.

The Grape that can with Logic absolute
The Two-and-Seventy jarring Sects confute:
    The subtle Alchemist that in a Trice
Life's leaden Metal into Gold transmute.

The mighty Mahmud, the victorious Lord,
That all the misbelieving and black Horde
    Of Fears and Sorrows that infest the Soul
Scatters and slays with his enchanted Sword.

But leave the Wise to wrangle, and with me
The Quarrel of the Universe let be:
    And In some corner of the Hubbub coucht,
Make Game of that which makes as much of Thee.

For In and out, above, about, below,
'T is nothing but a Magic Shadow-show,
    Play'd in a Box whose Candle is the Sun,
Round which we Phantom Figures come and go.

And if the Wine you drink, the Lip you press,
End in the Nothing all Things end in—Yes—
    Then fancy while Thou art, Thou art but what
Thou shalt be—Nothing—Thou shalt not be less.

While the Rose blows along the River Brink,
With old Khayyam the Ruby Vintage drink:
    And when the Angel with his darker Draught
Draws up to Thee—take that, and do not shrink.

'T is all a Chequer-board of Nights and Days
Where Destiny with Men for Pieces plays:
   Hither and thither moves, and mates, and slays,
And one by one back in the Closet lays.

The Ball no Question makes of Ayes and Noes,
But Right or Left, as strikes the Player, goes;
   And He that toss'd Thee down into the Field,
He knows about it all—HE knows—HE knows!

The Moving Finger writes; and, having writ,
Moves on: nor all thy Piety nor Wit
   Shall lure it back to cancel half a Line,
Nor all thy Tears wash out a word of it.

And that inverted Bowl we call The Sky,
Whereunder crawling coop't we live and die,
   Lift not thy hands to *It* for help—for it
Rolls impotently on as Thou or I.

With Earth's first Clay They did the Last Man's knead
And then of the Last Harvest sow'd the Seed:
   Yea, the first Morning of Creation wrote
What the Last Dawn of Reckoning shall read.

I tell Thee this—When starting from the Goal,
Over the shoulders of the flaming Foal
   Of Heav'n Parwin and Mushtari they flung,
In my predestin'd Plot of Dust and Soul —

The Vine had struck a Fibre; which about
If clings my Being—let the Sufi flout;
    Of my Base Metal may be filed a Key,
That shall unlock the Door he howls without.

And this I know: whether the one True Light,
Kindle to Love, or Wrath-consume me quite,
    One Glimpse of It within the Tavern caught
Better than in the Temple lost outright.

Oh, Thou, who didst with Pitfall and with Gin
Beset the Road I was to wander in,
    Thou wilt not with Predestination round
Enmesh me, and impute my Fall to Sin?

Oh, Thou, who Man of baser Earth didst make
And who with Eden didst devise the Snake;
    For all the Sin wherewith the Face of Man
Is blacken'd, Man's Forgiveness give—and take!

*   *   *   *   *   *   *   *   *

KÚZA-NÁMA.

LISTEN again.   One Evening at the Close
Of Ramazan, ere the better Moon arose,
    In that old Potter's Shop I stood alone
With the clay Population round in Rows.

And, strange to tell, among that Earthen Lot
Some could articulate, while others not:
     And suddenly one more impatient cried—
"Who *is* the Potter, pray, and who is the Pot?"

Then said another—"Surely not in vain
"My Substance from the common Earth was ta'en,
     "That He who subtly wrought me into Shape
"Should stamp me back to common Earth again."

Another said—"Why, ne'er a peevish Boy,
"Would break the Bowl from which he drank In Joy;
     "Shall He that *made* the Vessel in pure Love
"And Fansy, in after Rage destroy?"

None answered this; but after Silence spake
A Vessel of more ungainly Make:
     "They sneer at me for leaning all awry;
"What! did the Hand then of the Potter shake?"

Said one—"Folks of a surly Tapster tell,
"And daub his Visage with the Smoke of Hell;
     "They talk of some strict Testing of us—Pish!
"He's a Good Fellow, and 't will all be well."

Then said another with a long-drawn Sigh,
"My Clay with long oblivion is gone dry:
     "But, fill me with the old familiar Juice,
"Methinks I might recover by-and-bye!"

So while the Vessels one by one were speaking,
One spied the little Crescent all were seeking:
   And then they jogg'd each other, "Brother! Brother!
"Hark to the Porter's Shoulder-knot-a-creaking!"

*   *   *   *   *   *   *   *

Ah, with the Grape my fading Life provide,
And wash my Body whence the Life has died,
   And in the Winding-sheet of Vine-leaf wrapt,
So bury me by some sweet Garden-side.

That ev'n my buried Ashes such a Snare
Of Perfume shall fling up into the Air,
   As not a True Believer passing by
But shall be overtaken unaware.

Indeed the Idols I have loved so long
Have done my Credit in Men's Eye much wrong:
   Have drown'd my Honour in a shallow Cup,
And sold my Reputation for a Song.

Indeed, indeed, Repentance oft before
I swore—but was I sober when I swore?
   And then and then came Spring, and Rose-in-hand
My thread-bare Penitence apieces tore.

And much as Wine has played the Infidel,
And robbed me of my Robe of Honour—well,
   I often wonder what the Vintners buy
One-half so precious as the Goods they sell.

Alas, that Spring should vanish with the Rose!
That Youth's sweet-scented Manuscript should close!
   The Nightingale that in the Branches sang,
Ah, whence, and whither flown again, who knows!

Ah Love! could thou and I with Fate conspire
To grasp this sorry Scheme of Things entire,
   Would not we shatter it to bits—and then
Re-mould it nearer to the Heart's Desire.

Ah, Moon of my Delight who know'st no wane,
The Moon of Heav'n is rising once again:
   How oft hereafter rising shall she look
Through this same Garden after me—in vain!

And when Thyself with shining Foot shalt pass
Among the Guests Star-scatter'd on the Grass,
   And in thy joyous Errand reach the Spot
Where I made one—turn down an empty Glass!

TAMAM SHUD.

www.ingramcontent.com/pod-product-compliance
Lightning Source LLC
Chambersburg PA
CBHW022028080426
42733CB00007B/771